Traverse City
Then and Now –
A Photo History

Written by Bob Wilhelm

Also by Bob Wilhelm: *"Queen City" Barns, Carriage House and Neighborhoods,* 2011

Published 2016 by
Traverse Area Historical Society
PO Box 7051
Traverse City, MI 49696-7051

ISBN-10: 0-9983092-0-6
ISBN-13: 978-0-9983092-0-0

Cover composite photo created by Kayla Schopieray:
Sixth Street Carnegie Library building under construction in 1904 and current view.

Photo credit: Craig Bridson, Curator Fife Lake Historical Society
"The Traverse City Carnegie Library under construction, 1904"

Table of Contents

Dedication

We proudly dedicate this book to individuals who lived and preserved he history, events and memories of Traverse City, Michigan.

Harold "Doc" Aeschliman – Parks Superintendent, Miniature City expert. He lived and knew the stories of the east side.

Al Barnes – Photographed our history. He researched, wrote and preserved the memories of our backwood communities.

Bill Brown – "Mayor of South Union Street." Longtime printer for the Record-Eagle until his retirement in 1939. He lived and told the stories of the Union Street neighborhood.

Carol Hale – Historic preservationist, especially of the State Hospital and Traverse City Historic Districts.

Julius Petertyl – One hundred-three years of Bohemian and Central Neighborhood history.

Clayton Sporre – Preserved and chronicled local historic events.

Alexander (Alec) McCray Rennie – He lived and told the stories of the lumber era. His grandfather, William Rennie, was the "Bull of the Woods." He worked and bossed the Hannah Lay Camps and other Boardman Valley lumber operations.

Larry Wakefield – Writer of local history.

Thank you to these individuals and others who have preserved our history.

Robert D. Wilhelm

Preface

Cities change, but remnants of them survive, treasured reminders to those who care about history. Traverse City Then and Now *is intended to illuminate what used to be in our beloved city: the old gas plant now a candle store, an opera house barely changed from a century ago, an asylum now a thriving commercial and residential center, a candy factory now a popular site for drink and recreation, an abandoned theater now revived in a modern age. We need to remember the previous uses of transformed places like these, but so, too, do we need to remember the places forever gone, replaced by new things or never replaced at all: old train stations next to residences, a miniature city scattered in museums, countless factories long gone, frame buildings burned in an era before fire codes had been written.*

It is possible, as you walk close to our history – either by reading this book or by approaching a historical landmark—to imagine life eighty or hundred years ago, to smell the odor of horse manure and the exhaust of primitive autos, to see women in their long dresses and men in their overcoats, to dodge the bicyclists who raced through the streets, to hear the gongs of a fire alarm and the shrieks of passenger boats along the Bay. You can imagine waiting at the railroad station on Union Street; walking to Central High School with books under your arm, eating popcorn at the circus grounds, or ice skating on the Bay at a time when it froze solid almost every winter. Past time is constructed by our imaginations: let this book be a guide.

Enjoy *Traverse City Then and Now*. Dream and think about how our community used to be. Visit the old sites and look for relics all around you. As you walk the city, the past emerges from the bricks and mortar of places nearby, the ancient trees of old neighborhoods, the cinders that fell from steam-powered locomotives. History exists only when we vision it Let us not forget to imagine.

Richard Fidler, 2013

Acknowledgements

Dave Pennington, *volunteer, History Center of Traverse City*

Amy Hansen, *Revolution Design & Printing*

Peg Siciliano, *Archivist, History Center of Traverse City*

Bruce Wiegand, *photographer, editor and former Board Member of History Center of Traverse City*

The Traverse Area Historical Society Publications Committee, *editing and photographs*

Introduction

Traverse City Then and Now developed from discussion between the author and others at the History Center of Traverse City and the Traverse Area District Library. TADL displayed twelve "Then and Now" exhibits over a three-year period. At some point it became evident that a book of these images would be appropriate. I thank the Traverse Area District Library and History Center of Traverse City for all of their assistance.

I would also like to note four Traverse City citizens who were instrumental in recording the area's past:

Perry Hannah, the "Father of Traverse City," took great pride in the growth of "his" city from the 1850s until his death in 1904.

Newspapers are a major source for information on this period. In 1858 Morgan Bates founded the *Grand Traverse Herald*. Along with this "anti-slavery crusade" he also published a history of Traverse City. Morgan Bates' nephew, Thomas T. Bates, became general manager of the *Herald*. He continued to record the area's history and also took great interest in law and order, and in the temperance movement.

In 1866 Elvin Sprague moved the *Elk Rapids Eagle* to Traverse City and began publishing the *Traverse Bay Eagle*. His "History of Grand Traverse and Leelanau Counties, Michigan's Review of Their Early Settlers" was a description of life in the region is an important resource even today.

Stephen E. Wait has been called Traverse City's renaissance man. He was a man of many skills – educator, carpenter, clerk & steward aboard the "City of Traverse," druggist, and a meteorologist who reported to the Smithsonian. His photographs have been preserved for the modern generation. They are a valuable visual resource for today's historians and researchers.

We mention four who played an early part in historic preservation, but there are many others. To these people, we say thank you!

The Author

+ Dr. James Decker Munson was the first superintendent at the Northern Michigan Asylum, which opened in 1885. The center building housed the superintendent's office and residence. Administration offices, and patient services were also in this center building.

+ Spreading out from this center building were eighteen halls serving patients with various mental disorders. Those with short-term, mild disorders lived nearest to the center. The most disturbed were housed on the farthest halls.

+ The center building was condemned in the early 1960s. An elegant, open staircase was a major problem due to fire concerns. The building was removed in 1963.

+ A modern, state designed office building replaced the historic structure.

+ Today Building 50 is owned by the Minervini Group of developers. A restaurant, shops, offices, apartments and condominiums are in this building.

In 1915 after fire destroyed the only general hospital in the area, Dr. James G. Munson opened an unused building at the State Hospital on the corner of Eleventh Street and Elmwood Avenue for use as a general hospital. The building had been the residence of an early settler, Charles Chantler. In the early 1880s it served as a boarding house for the masons, carpenters, and other tradesmen who were building the Northern Michigan Asylum. By the early 1920s the building could not accommodate the demand for patient care and a new, modern hospital was built a block to the north using local and state funds. Over the years the hospital has expanded to become what is today Munson Medical Center.

The 2nd Elmwood school pictured here was built in 1892, serving Slabtown and adjoining neighborhoods. Following World War II the community voted to replace two outdated schools – Oak Park and Elmwood. This old building and an adjacent gymnasium were demolished in 1956, with Willow Hill School opening in the neighboring foothills. The property was sold by the school district and the neighborhood gained several additional homes.

The waterfront along West Grand Traverse Bay was a cluttered mess in the late 1800s and early 1900s. Waste lumber from the Hannah & Lay, Greilick and other mills piled up. Workers returning from a day's work picked up slab lumber and built their homes with it.

The original Slabtown neighborhood was bordered by Front, Division, Bay and Gillis Streets, although today the term also refers to the neighborhood west of Division. The mostly Bohemian residents had little money, so using slabs for their homes was a real boon. A reconstructed home at 508 Second Street may be the last standing slab home in this area. In the later twentieth century, siding was removed during renovation, and a slab house was found underneath. Czech language newspapers were pasted to the inner walls, placed there to keep the wind from blowing between the cracks. Are there any more hidden gems behind the modern faces of these historic homes?

Slabtown also boasted a commercial district. There was a Bohemian Club (the C.S. P.S.) on Oak and Front and several businesses on Randolph Street – Kroupa Saloon, Stephan Market ("Fresh Salt and Smoked Meat"), Sladek Tailors and the Chervenka bakery all in the 500 block. The John Kauer saloon, built in 1905, was at 601 Randolph where Bay Bread is now located.

+ The oldest continuously operating tavern in Traverse City opened in 1882. It had taken three years to build, as crews worked only on Sunday, because they had to work elsewhere the other six days. The ceiling is stamped tin. Walls are lined with memorabilia, much of it from the Victorian Era, with hunting trophies looking down on the patrons.

+ The original bar is in use today, although the spittoons lining the front are gone. During prohibition the second-generation Louis Sleder openly sold soft drinks and lunches. In reality the tavern also was a "Blind Pig," with free drinks to the police, the mayor and a judge. The tavern certainly wasn't dry. It was rumored that regular trips were made to Chicago to buy grain alcohol from the Capone gang. Necessary ingredients were added to concoct gin or other types of alcohol.

+ After more than 130 years, Sleder's Family Tavern retains most of the history and charm of by-gone days.

In 1926 Jerry Oleson took over his father's grocery store on West Front Street. This was the same year he married Frances Deering. In 1932 he built a larger, most modern store next door. When it opened it was the largest grocery store north of Grand Rapids. This building still stands. As his grocery chain expanded, Oleson became a buffalo farmer, land owner and philanthropist. He and is wife left their mark on Traverse City as have few other individuals.

In 1955 the Olesons provided funds for an annual barbecue fundraiser for education. That first year's funds were split between St. Francis High School, for the construction of a gymnasium, and Northwestern Michigan College. This event became an annual fundraiser for the college, and continues today.

Eventually Jerry and Frances eventually organized the Oleson Foundation. They were early contributors to Munson Medical Center, and strong supporters of the Boy Scouts and other community groups. Frances passed away in 1994, Jerry in 1997 at the age of 91.

The Oleson Store at 902 West Front closed when a new, state of the art store opened on West Long Lake and Cedar Run Roads. A second new store opened at Hammond and Three Mile road, replacing the Olesons on Garfield Ave. Today the West Front Street building is occupied by imprés Salon and Spa. A doctor's office occupies the back of the building.

- A penniless immigrant from Bohemia, Ferdinand (Fred) Schall came to Traverse City in the early 1900s to work for a Bohemian bakery on Randolph Street. He started his own bakery in the 100 block of East Front Street before purchasing a site at 805 W. Front. Originally he operated a retail business, but later opened "Tasty" bread, a wholesale firm. The products were sold all over northwestern Michigan. The family sold the business in 1962 to Interstate Bakers (Butternut Bread).

- In 1998 the building – in need of repair – was remodeled into a retail and office complex.

In 1928 at the corner of W. Front and Oak, Louie Johnson operated the Red Crown Gasoline station. Louie and his wife Nettie lived upstairs. Other familiar names that operated stations at this site include Alf Rufli, Don Scammahon, Oscar Johnson and Edward Pokoj. Soon after a modern gas station opened on the former site of Madsen's Flowers at 507 E. Front Street, the Red Crown Gasoline station closed. After many years Modern Cleaners moved here from the 200 block of E. Front Street. Today Elite Cleaners and Jere's Barber Shop occupy the site.

ROLL OF HONOR

MEN AND WOMEN FROM GRAND TRAVERSE COUNTY

SPONSORED BY THE TRAVERSE CITY EXCHANGE CLUB

✢ Nearly two thousand names of Grand Traverse County servicemen and women were listed in the Exchange Club Roll of Honor raised in 1944. All of this work resulted from the belief that "a memorial should be erected to remind us of the sacrifices the boys are making on foreign soil."

✢ The fire department moved from its historic Cass Street building to its new building on this site in 1975. Originally the police department was in adjacent offices. They are now located with the Sheriff's department in the Law Center on Woodmere Avenue.

✢ The Fire Department's current neighbors are the Grand Traverse Commission on Aging and the Michigan State University Extension Service.

- ✛ Immigrants arriving in large numbers from Europe in the second half of the 19th century formed benevolent and protective societies. The Czech-Bohemians organized the CSPS (Ceko-Shovansky Pod Porujia Spolen) or Bohemian Social Club in a residence on West North Street. As membership grew the society moved to the 300 block of South Union Street. In 1906 the group built and moved to a larger building, pictured here, at the corner of Oak and Front Street.

- ✛ As older generations of immgrants died and later generations "Amer-canized," such ethnic organizations began to lose their importance.

- ✛ In the 1930s the building was sold to the Knights of Columbus. In 1945 it was sold to the Veterans of Foreign Wars. They left in 1990.

- ✛ After being vacant for a few years the building was renovated by Bishop and Heintz for their law office.

STRAUB BRO'S & AMIOTTE
HOME OF THE FAMOUS
S.B. & A. CHOCOLATES AND CANDIES

- Straub Brothers and Amiotte built their four-story candy factory in 1905. A railroad siding brought carloads of sugar, barrels of syrup, and nutmeats that were then stored in the basement. Many varieties of candies were produced over the next two decades.

- In the 1920s the industry moved from locally manufactured candy to nationally advertised packaged brands like Milky Way and Hershey.

- In 1928 Straub and Amiotte joined the marketing syndicate of Seal Crest Chocolate. The group was an early victim of the great depression when it went out of business. So did Straub Brothers & Amiotte.

- Many businesses have occupied this location, including Burwood Manufacturing, Fochtman Motor Company and a furniture store. Presently the upper floors are offices.

- North Peak Brewing Company and Kilkenneys Irish Public House occupy the main floor and lower level.

In the early twentieth century the area between 12th and 14th, Pine and Wadsworth streets was cleared of lumber. It became the circus grounds and the early fair grounds. Circus trains would roll into the twelfth street Pere Marquette yards and set up there. A circus parade would wind through downtown before the performances at the circus grounds. Many circuses came to town, including Buffalo Bill's Wild West Show and Ringling Brothers. The first fair was held in 1908. Admission was 25 cents. By 1912 the City was growing and a new fair site was necessary. The fair moved to East Front street, what is today the Grand Traverse Civic Center.

After 1912, the area was often used as a football field by Traverse City High School. During the 1920s and '30s a fence was constructed around the field so that admission to the games could be charged. In 1934 the Athletic Board of Control decided to build a new athletic. The field was rebuilt, and bleachers, a press box, scoreboard and running track were added. In recognition of his long support and dedication of area sports, the new facility was named in honor of Dr. E.L. Thirlby. In 1937 lighting was installed.

Thirlby Field was in need of repair in the early 2000s. The estate of lawyer Harry Running provided initial funds to build new grandstands. Funds from the Oleson Foundation provided the press box. Donations from sports sponsors "Between the Fences" enabled the facilities to be complete. The Fences allowed the Thirlby Field renovations to be completed. Don and Gerry Oleson also underwrote the installation of artificial turf. Today the Harry Running Stadium at Thirlby Field is one of the outstanding athletic facilities in Michigan.

+ Neighborhood gas stations were located throughout the city before and after World War II. Clune Heiges operated a Sinclair gas station at the corner of Front and Wadsworth streets. Many of these stations were picturesque. Crandall Brothers at Eighth and Union was one of the most unique. It was the second gas station in Michigan to be designated a state historic landmark. Several "doll house" Sinclair gas stations were constructed throughout the area.

+ Today the gas pumps are long gone. The Flower Station thrives on this site.

In the late 19th century the city streets were dark and dangerous, although on a clear night the moon could illuminate the area. Candles could light the homes. Better lighting became available in the 1880s as Thomas Edison's dynamo produced alternating current incandescent lighting. Boardman River Electric Light and Power Company, "The House of Electric Service," was opened in 1893 serving the downtown area and later spreading throughout the neighborhoods.

In competition, The Traverse City Gas Company – "If done with heat you can do better with gas" – opened in 1901. It never garnered popularity. The gas produced was coal gas. The large bell tank. Floating in liquid, raised as it filled with gas produced in the factory.

The gas produced was dirty and spread soot, covering much of the area. The ugly smell was overwhelming. The city fathers and the population constantly complained. The days of gas production were declining, and the business closed around 1930.

Vacant for several decades, the dirty, decrepit building seemed beyond repair. In the early 1970s the slow cleaning process began and the Candle Factory opened.

✛ On June 29, 1892 the first Manistee and North Eastern passenger train arrived at the new depot. It was built on land donated by Perry Hannah. Passengers and lumber was the main source of business at first. The hope was that farm produce, especially potatoes, would replace the declining lumber trade. That hope diminished, for after two or three plantings the fertile soil was gone.

✛ The railroad struggled financially until it declared bankruptcy. In 1932 the Pere Marquette Railroad took control and in 1934 the mainline from Kaleva to Solon was abandoned. For several years the abandoned depot was a warehouse, then demolished in 1948.

✛ The 1996 Traverse City Visitor Center replicates the exterior of the old depot.

In the early twentieth century, like many other urban waterfronts, Traverse City was cluttered with factories, railroads and numerous run-down structures. The clutter began to disappear as Grandview Parkway opened in the early 1950s. With the coming of the highway, US-31 followed the Parkway, leaving behind the traffic-filled Front and Union streets.

Disappearing from the waterfront were the Grand Rapids and Indiana (Pennsylvania) Railroad. and the Manistee and Northeastern, Railroad. Industrial buildings went down as well, such as Musselman's Grocery Supplies, Rickards Storage and Fuel, Morgan Cherry Products, and Ginsburg Iron and Metal. The last industrial structure – the large – electric generating plant, came down in 2000.

The Hannah-Lay Coal Dock was cleared of run-down buildings and railroad tracks, the cleared area becoming today's Open Space. In addition, most of the bayfront from Front Street to the Leelanau County line has been cleared and landscaping has helped make the waterfront more attractive.

Con Foster Museum, Clinch Park, Traverse City, Mich.

✛ Con Foster, a former employee of the Barnum and Bailey Circus, came to Traverse City in 1925 as manager of the Lyric Theater. Finding a waterfront that was an industrial wasteland, he campaigned for a cleanup. In 1930 he suggested that the waterfront be used for a park and aquarium. Within three days he raised $3,000 from private individuals to start construction. Federal Funds from the Civil Works Administration helped finish the project.

✛ In1935, Con Foster realized his grandest dream: the founding of a new museum, the Con Foster Museum. In his last years, he traveled the country collecting artifacts for the museum. This collection is presently housed in the old library on Sixth Street, currently occupied by the Crooked Tree Arts Center.

✛ With the exception of a few temporary summer activities, the building sat empty for many years, but in 2013 the Traverse City Film Festival, under the leadership of filmmaker Michael Moore, with seed money provided by Richard and Diana Milock, offered to renovate and restore this historic building into a year-round movie house: Bijou By The Bay.

+ Perry Hannah's first bank opened in 1856 on Bay Street near the Boardman River. In the 1880's the bank was located at the company's headquarters in the Hannah-Lay Building, currently standing at the corner of Union and Front streets. It started as part of the Chicago-based Safety Vault Company, but in 1892 it was incorporated as the Traverse City State Bank. The bank outgrew its location and in 1903 Perry Hannah hired Chicago architect H.H. Waterman to design a new bank building. Perry Hannah, himself, is said to have placed the cornerstone of the new structure on the northwest corner of Front and Union Streets. The bank opened in1904. Its hallmark was a lofty tower that displayed a Seth Thomas four-faced clock which was purchased through local jeweler J. N. Martinek.

+ The bank continued to expand, surviving the Great Depression. By 1981 changes in the banking industry led to a merger of Traverse City State Bank, the conglomerate called Pacemaker Bank and Trust. After two more mergers, the bank became 5/3 Bank, the name it bears today (2016).

In 1901 Emmanuel Wilhelm announced plans to build the town's first "skyscraper" – a five-story retail and office building. Many conservative businessmen "doubted the wisdom of the undertaking in a town of this size." On March 15, 1902 "Mr. Wilhelm had a grand opening of his dry goods and clothing store which occupies the first floor with large display windows." The upper floors were offices, which had high occupancies. Despite the initial optimism, the business failed in 1909. In 1910 Emmanuel Wilhelm was elected as the first Democrat mayor of Traverse City. He was defeated in 1912. He was appointed Postmaster in 1915 and served for ten years.

Fire was always a problem in this building. After conversion to the Hotel Traverse there were several small blazes, and a major fire where Leona Way was killed when she missed the blanket held by several men. Fire partially destroyed the building on November 15, 1970 and subsequently the upper three floors were removed.

Today retail stores occupy the ground floor, with offices on the second floor.

- As early as 1878 Perry Hannah had plans to build a mammoth brick department store to replace several wooden stores on Union Street between the Bay and Boardman River.

- Ground for the Hannah and Lay Mercantile Company was broken on March 26, 1883. More than two million bricks from Markham Brick Yards on Cedar Lake were used. The mercantile store "Dealer in Every Thing," "Universal Provider," stayed in business until 1929.

- A variety of tenants, including a furniture store, occupied the building until 1939 when most of the store was taken over by Montgomery Ward.

- A massive fire on April 16, 1940 destroyed the eastern two sections the hardware store, with exploding paints and bullets creating an Independence Day atmosphere. A firewall probably saved the rest of the building. Montgomery Ward left downtown December 24, 1980.

- In recent years a sports shop and a bank are on the ground floor. Offices fill the upper floors.

- In 2013 the Hannah, Lay & Co. building was listed as a state historical landmark.

The four-story Masonic Temple was constructed in 1890. The upper two floors were used for Temple activities. The second floor was offices, and the ground floor was rented for businesses. S. E. Wait's Pioneer Drug Store and the Post Office were the earliest occupants. When the Post Office moved, Frank Trude opened a hardware store, a business that lasted for 80 years. Another business was the City News Company. L.M. Bennett sold watches, clocks and jewelry. The offices of Michigan Telephone Company and the Old Mission Stage Line were on the second floor. In 1987 a fire destroyed the upper two floors. Instead of demolishing the badly damaged building, it was rebuilt as a three-floor office and retail structure. The oldest continuous business in the Masonic building is Robertson's Barber Shop. Major Robertson opened his business in 1912. The Masonic Temple moved to a new site in 1976.

- With a population of nearly 5,000 in 1889 Traverse City needed a meeting place. A few churches and the Ladies Library on the second floor of an old wooden building on Front Street offered very small spaces for community meetings. About this time, three brothers-in-law, Charles Wilhelm, Anton Bartak and Frank Votruba needed more room for their growing grocery and harness-making businesses.

- At the urging of Perry Hannah, they were asked to build a three-story building with stores on the ground floor. Eventually, plans for a 1200-seat theater were proposed. On April 6, 1891 ground was broken.

- A vacant lot between the Opera House and the Masonic Temple was purchased. A fourth business on the ground floor and a third floor lodge for the Maccabees were constructed. The second floor was an academy where musicians could practice.

- In addition to plays and banquets, other activities took place. These included basketball games, donkey basketball and Prof. D. M. Bristol's Horse Show! In 1920 the Fitzpatrick and McElroy Movie Theater Company leased the Opera House and closed it in an effort to eliminate competition.

- In 1972 the City Opera House was placed on the National Register of Historical Places. William and Gretchen Votruba donated the Opera House to the city and people of Traverse City in 1980.

- In 1981 the City Opera House Heritage Committee signed a lease to manage and restore the opera house.

- In 2009 the City Opera House Association signed a three-year agreement with the Wharton Center for Performing Arts to manage in partnership. World-class entertainment arrived: Jazz at Lincoln Center with Wynton Marsalis, Lily Tomlin, and Frank d'Ambrosio. Despite early problems, things got worked out. The *Record-Eagle* editorial stated: "Wharton, Opera House prove a winning combination."

F. W. WOOLWORTH CO.
5 AND 10 CENT STORE

CAFE

+ Peter Wurzburg built this three-story building in 1890 and opened Beers and Wurzburg Furniture. He became the city treasurer after closing the business in the early 1900s. The F.W. Woolworth Co. "10¢ store" occupied the space until 1932.

+ Milton "Butch" Petertyl operated his Walgreen Agency Drug Store there until 1978 when the store moved across the street. Stewart-Zacks Fabrics moved in, and restored and enhanced the period design of the exterior.

+ Brilliant Books is the present business on the ground floor.

MICHIGAN
THEATRE

NOW PLAYING
JEAN ARTHUR in
THE DEVIL and MISS JONES

Opening
NEXT WEDNESDAY
Jean Arthur in the
DEVIL & MISS JONES

- The days of vaudeville and other live theater live entertainment came to an end as the twentieth century progressed and moving pictures arrived.

- The Palace Ice Cream Parlor and Palace Picture Show opened at 128 E. Front Street in 1904. There were several other theaters on Front Street, including the Dreamland, which offered movies and a live performance from the manager, "Yours Truly, G. Lote Silver."

- Other names graced movie theaters, including the Star, Electric Theatre, Travis, Tra-Bay and Lyric. The names are gone, but memories remain.

- In the early 1940s, the Butterfield Theater Chain built the modern air-conditioned, one-thousand-seat Michigan Theater. In the basement was a bowling alley. In 1958 the Moonlight Gardens Roller Rink replaced the bowling alley.

- Television and urban sprawl brought the days of downtown theaters to a close. In 1980 the Michigan Theater was closed. Its large marquee and balcony were removed.

- In 1982 Front Row Centre opened as a combination of offices. Stores are at street level and the ECCO Event Space is below.

- In 1868 two young men left Maine to seek their fortune in the west. J. W. Milliken and Frank Hamilton arrived in Traverse City and began working for Hannah & Lay. In 1873, with support from Perry Hannah, the two young men opened Hamilton, Milliken & Co. selling dry goods and apparel. At the turn of the 20th century the store became two separate but connected businesses. The decision was friendly – Hamilton chose menswear and Milliken concentrated his efforts on a department store. The Milliken business modernized and expanded during the next eighty years. One of the most popular additions was the balcony tea room. It was often called the city's best-kept secret." Everything from soup to nuts was homemade.

- The Milliken family sold the landmark business in 1983.

- On January 4, 2001 it was announced that the current occupant, the womens clothing store Stage Milliken would close within 60 to 90 days. This would be the end of a 128-year tradition.

- Milliken Place, a renovated structure with stores and offices "built to last another 120 years," opened in 2002. The design of the new facade was influenced by historic photos and the desire to make the building's appearance both fit in to the surrounding area and serve as a focal point on an important street corner.

MARTINEK'S JEWELERS
WRIGHT'S DRUGS
CUT RATE
CUT RATE
3 Photos 10

In the 1930s and 1940s, familiar stores on the north side of this block were the Little Tavern, Wright's Cut-Rate Drugs, S.S. Kresge, Martinek Jewelers and Hopkins. Beyond was the Elks Club, which burned in 1963, and the remains of Steinburg's Opera House.

Today the familiar stores of the past are gone, being replaced by shops catering to tourists and townspeople.

+ Today, if you stand on the southwest corner of Cass and Front Streets and look down the south side of the tree-lined street, you will see several thriving businesses – first, a small park, then Cherry Hill Boutique, Talbots, the Whiting Hotel and Cherry Republic.

+ Step back fifty or a hundred years, and the scene transforms. Businesses then included Dahlquists 5 & 10 (and before that Prokop Kyselkas) Curtis and Roosa Shoes, Coddington Music, the Whiting Hotel, Wolverine Café, Sleder's Meat Market, B.F. Comstock and Roxburgh Rexall Drugs.

MILLER BROS
CLOTHING

+ Harness-maker John T. Beadle rented a shop at the northwest corner of Front and Cass Streets in 1873. In 1888 Perry Hannah sold the site to Beadle. In 1892 Beadle built the "imposing three-story building bearing his name." There were several offices in the upper floors.

+ Grinnell Bros., "Michigan's leading music house, selling everything musical," became an occupant. Bageno's Appliance Shop, selling gifts, appliances, floor coverings, Pyrofax gas, books, furniture, and paints was in business there in the 1940s and '50s. Cunningham drug store was next, with a modern renovation.

+ In 1985 the exterior was restored to its 19th century architecture by Elias Brothers Restaurant, "Home of the Big Boy."

+ The present-day occupant is Mackinaw Brewing Company, retaining the turn of the century appearance.

+ Traverse City's first organized fire department was founded on May 6, 1897. Funds were raised to purchase hose carts. These two hose carts were named the "Invincible" and "Wide Awake." The department operated in a one-story wooden shack on the 200 block of Front Street, now the location of Amical Restaurant. The editor of the *Grand Traverse Herald* Thomas T. Bates stated, "The old fire hall was nothing more than a firetrap." He urged a vote to issue bonds for $5,000 to build a brick firehouse. Construction at 120 Cass Street began in August 1891 and was completed five months later at a cost of $4,000.

+ In the early 1900s the city owned two horse-drawn steamers, a hook and ladder and two hose carts. The four paid firemen were also authorized policemen.

+ The fire alarm consisted of a long "mockingbird" call, followed by short whistles to identify the location. Seven short blasts indicated that the fire was extinguished.

+ The first gasoline-powered engines came between 1917 and 1920.

+ In July 1975 Fire Station One closed and the new station at 510 W. Front Street was opened. Over the next 40 years several restaurants and retail establishments opened and closed. The present business is the French restaurant, Bistro Foufou.

- Julius Steinberg came to the United States after escaping from Russian-controlled Poland. He arrived in Traverse City in 1868, working as a peddlar walking from farm to farm with all his goods on his back. He spoke very little English but quickly learned the power of "please," "Hello, please," "Good-bye please." He soon bought a horse and wagon and later opened a dry goods and clothing business on Front Street.

- As his wealth increased, he purchased one hundred feet of property on the north side of Front Street. In 1891 he began construction of a highly-ornamented building for his business and opera house. On December 11, 1897 with Steinberg and his family in their private box, the curtain rose for the first time. The production was "Hamlet."

- As the years passed the theater earned the praise of the community with high class prsentations and well-known entertainers.

- By 1910 opera houses began to lose their appeal. The age of motion pictures was taking over. The 900-seat opera house closed in 1915. The Steinberg store closed in 1922 following the death of Jake Steinberg, the son of Julius.

- Fires destroying the adjacent Lyric Theatre and the Elks Club weakening the upper walls of the Opera House. Today Amical Restaurant occupies the site of the Steinberg store.

LYRIC

Fitzpatrick
McElroy
Company

"THE LIGHT
THAT FAILED" #
GUSHER COMEDY

As the days of the opera house came to a close, in 1913 the Steinburgs built the Lyric Theater next to their opera house. The theater burned in 1923, but soon was rebuilt. In the 1930s a former circus man for Barnum & Bailey, Con Foster, was the manager. The theater burned again in 1948.

After rebuilding, it re-opened as the State Theater in 1949. Like so many the theaters throughout the country, it was eventually remodeled to hold two screens in an attempt to remain viable. Even with this effort it was closed for several years.

The rebirth of the theater occurred in 2004 with the start of the Traverse City Film Festival. Michael Moore, John Robert Williams and Doug Stanton led this effort. Today it is a showcase of the city, named #1 in a 2013 global top–ten listing of cinemas.

TRAVERSE CITY BUSINESS COLLEGE

- Professor Charles Dockery opened the Traverse City Business College in the early 1900s. "Bookkeeping, Shorthand and Typewriting a Specialty" was the college slogan. Dr. James Decker Munson, Superintendent at the Northern Michigan Asylum, built the building. It was one of several downtown buildings which he built or managed.

- In later years Gambles used the ground floor, and Miller apartments occupied the upper floors.

- The popular Red Ginger restaurant now occupies the building.

✛ The headline in the October 27, 1926
Traverse City Record Eagle announced.
"Bldg. Opens Thursday." J. C. Penney
opened a landmark store that remained
in the location for more than 60 years.
In 1998 it moved to the newly opened
Grand Traverse Mall. In September 1992
Vic Herman announced plans to purchase
the Penney building and move his Horizon
Book Store from across the street. Moving
day came and volunteers gathered on a
Sunday morning to move the contents
from the old location to the far larger
Penney building. Today the Horizon Book
Store is a community gathering spot, café
and music venue.

CITIES
SERVICE

CITIES
SERVICE

GAS

CITIES SERVIC

Before US-31 was moved from Front Street to Grandview Parkway in the early 1950's there were several gas stations downtown. Today there are none. At the corner of Front and Park Streets there were three stations: Firestone at the northwest corner, Standard Oil at the southeast corner and Cities Service on the northeast corner. Cities Service was replaced by the Bean Pot restaurant. It is now the site of the Dingeman & Dancer law offices.

+ Small town breweries were being built steadily across the United States as the frontier moved west. In 1901 Joseph Gambs, a Milwaukee brewmaster, built the city's first brewery at 719 E. Front Street. The Traverse City Brewing Company was incorporated in 1903 with Gambs as president and Peter Wurzburg as treasurer. By 1908 the Sleder brothers, Louis and Andrew, were largely involved in the Brewing Company and sold the locally made beer in their tavern on Randolph St. The brewery was closed during Prohibition. It later became part of Cherry Growers canning company.

+ The brewery building and other Cherry Growers buildings were used by Northwestern Michigan College until they were demolished to make way for the NMC Great Lakes campus. The brewery was located near today's George and Clara McManus Building.

In 1895 John C. Morgan arrived in Traverse City to manage Hannah and Lay's cider mill. A year later he went into business for himself. As his mill on the bayfront expanded, production grew from cider to include other apple and cherry products.

John "Cider" Morgan bought this 1894 residence in 1904. The house was in the family for three generations. When John Morgan died it passed to his son Don S. Morgan and then to Mary Morgan Linsley, who died in 1960.

Now called Sunnybank, it is the home of Joe and Dee Blair and has been beautifully remodeled and restored.

Built on the site of the first city cemetery, the Carnegie Library opened in 1905. In 1902 Andrew Carnegie had offered the City $20,000 to build a library if the city would pledge $2,000 a year for library expenses, and provide an adequate site. A controversy erupted over which property to use. Land ranging from $2,000 to $6,000 was offered for sale to the City. Perry Hannah offered free land with no strings attached. His offer was originally declined because the site was not centrally located. Two years of bitter debates and a lawsuit did not solve the problem. Mayor John Santo even suggested that the money be returned if the disputes continued. Finally, on May 11, 1903, the City Council approved the Hannah site. It was not until March 7, 1904 that the final lawsuit was thrown out of court.

In May 1904, ground was broken in what is now Hannah Park. The library opened March 10, 1905. It boasted a collection of 7,000 books, most of which came from the Ladies' Library. In 1966 an 8,000 square-foot addition was built to the east. The library closed December 20, 1998 and moved to its then-new Boardman Lake campus.

On June 27th, 2002, after a $1.4 million renovation, the city-owned Carnegie Library building reopened as the Grand Traverse Heritage Center, then later, the History Center of Traverse City, which managed the city's Con Foster museum collection until 2014. The building now houses the Crooked Tree Arts Center.

+ In retirement by 1893, Perry Hannah moved from his modest home near the bay to a lavish Queen Ann residence on Sixth Street. It cost $40,000. The estimated replacement cost today is $3 million. Hannah lived in the house for eleven years until his death in 1904.

+ Perry's son Julius and his wife Elsie were the next residents. Julius died in 1905 of a ruptured appendix and Elsie lived there until 1933. Elsie donated the house to the American Legion, although it was never used as their headquarters. In 1934, when Central Elementary School burned, classes were held in the house.

+ In 1936 the home was purchased by Harry Weaver and opened as the H. L. Weaver Funeral Home. Floyd Reynolds took over in 1949 and it became the Reynolds Funeral Home. Twenty years later Fred Hanson purchased it. Jack and Dan Jonkhoff acquired the property January 1, 1976. Six years later it was renamed the Reynolds-Jonkhoff Funeral Home. In 1992 Dan and Peg Jonkhoff purchased the property and business. Today Perry Hannah's retirement home is the Reynolds-Jonkhoff Funeral Home, a National Registered Landmark.

OLD SETTLERS REST ROOM

PATRIOTIC
BAND CONCERT
HERE TONIGHT

OLD SETTLERS
◄ WELCOME ►
REST AND REGISTER

LIVERY

PATRIOTIC
BAND CONCERT

- The Old Settlers Association was organized in 1884. Membership was open to anyone who had lived in Grand Traverse, Leelanau, Antrim, Kalkaska, Charlevoix counties for more than twenty years.

- In 1916 the Old Settlers purchased a structure at Front and Cass Streets from the Board of Trade. It was a "comfort station" (restrooms). This became the Settlers' headquarters and a place to preserve photographs. Members would meet here for conversation, storytelling and occasional "tall tales."

- Band concerts were held there. The Grand Traverse Auto Company Military Band was a frequent guest. Occasionally rooftop performances were given.

- The building was eventually moved to 206 Union Street. The final journey of the clubhouse was to Twelfth Street, near today's Thirlby Field. It was used as a warming house for the skating rink.

RENNIE OIL CO.

The PIONEER STATION OF THE NORTH

TIRE SALE

U.S. ROYAL

+ In the early 1900s, the northwest corner of State and Union Streets was considered the busiest corner in town. Potato buyers met sellers and conducted their business under the trees.

+ It seemed like a great location when Charles Rennie opened the Pioneer Station of the North there in 1919. It was the first modern gasoline station to be built north of Grand Rapids, and it sat on what was then the State Highway.

+ With the opening of the Grandview Parkway as the new state route in 1952, business declined for all the downtown stations. However, this business remained.

+ In 1971 Clint Kinney purchased the station. It remained in his family when the business closed and moved to Grawn.

+ The Bank of Northern Michigan opened at this site with an award-winning three-floor office building in 2006.

TRAVERSE CITY WAGON WORKS.

A. J. PETERTYL.

HORSE SHOEING

+ In 1894 A. J. Petertyl bought property at the southwest corner of State and Union Streets and built the A. J. Petertyl Wagon Works, later renamed the Traverse City Wagon Works. An early ad states:
  "Manufacturers of all kinds of delivery wagons, trucks, lumber wagons. Delivery, farm and logging sleighs with our patent, a specialty general forging, horse shoeing, and carriage painting. Manufacturers of sanitary Cherry Pickers."

+ In 1917, "Tony" retired because of health problems and sold his business to nephews and longtime employees, the Slaby brothers.

+ By the 1920s, the Traverse City Post Office which stood at the corner of State and Cass Streets, had become too small to handle the increasing volume of mail. During the Depression many post offices were being built with Works Progress Administration funds, and Traverse City was on the list.

+ Construction of the new building began in 1937, with the Post Office opening in September 1939. An addition was built in 1964.

- ⊹ Hannah Lay opened its gristmill on the west side of Cass Street, just south of the Boardman River, in 1868. Originally steam was used to grind the wheat and other crops brought in by local farmers.

- ⊹ Later three water-powered turbines powered the mill. One hundred barrels of flour were produced daily. Bags of Hannah's Best Flour and Turkey Red were familiar sights.

- ⊹ On January 26, 1926 the mill was destroyed by fire. For years the only remains were the mill's foundation. This was demolished in a later landscaping project.

- ⊹ Today landscaping has hidden the mill site. A small dam for the upstream movement of fish is visible. Condominiums border the riverside.

- The first Chicago & West Michigan train arrived in Traverse City in 1890, stopping near the waterfront at Park Street, as the depot on Union Street was not yet finished.

- A. W. Wait had the contract to build all railroad structures from Baldwin to Traverse City. The Traverse City Depot opened at a cost of $2,500.

- The nearby freight house (which still stands at the corner of Cass and Lake Streets, (today the Om Cafe) opened at a cost of $1500.

- In 1926 the Pere Marquette built a new depot on Railroad Avenue. As that building was on the mainline, the passenger train no longer had to back in as it did at Union Street Depot. This improvement cut as much as an hour off the schedule. The old depot was moved to Cass and Twelfth Street to be used as a warehouse and demolished in 1956.

- Lay Park, named in honor of founding father A. Tracy Lay is on the site today.

+ In the mid- to late- nineteenth century, several northern Michigan iron works were built to repair and construct parts for the lumber companies. In 1871 W.F. Calkins and Benjamin Thirlby founded the Traverse City Iron Works and H.G. Joynt was hired as plant superintendent. The firm continued to grow, expanding its product line. Joynt designed and patented the "Traverse City Iron Works all weather fire hydrant." It provided a hydraulic no-freeze water shut-off below the frost line.

+ In 1964 almost all the business was from hydrants, valves and fittings. In 1973 the firm expanded with a 52,000 square foot foundry that exceeded all state and Federal pollution standards. It was located in the Industrial Park.

+ In 1977 the Iron Works was sold to Amhoist of St. Paul, Minnesota, In 1983 the business closed, throwing all 118 employees out of work.

+ Today, other than a chrome fire hydrant on Cass Street, all of the remains of the original iron works are gone. Condominiums and the world headquarters for Hagerty Insurance occupy the site.

+ Around 1880 Jane Shilson built the Boardman River House at the corner of Union Street and Lake Avenue. Her son Thomas became the manager on his twenty-first birthday. He later became the owner. The hotel catered mainly to salesmen who arrived at the nearby Pere Marquette Depot. The large dining room, known as the Eating House, catered to the guests and Mrs. Shilson was the cook. No alcoholic beverages were allowed. For those, the salesmen would go next door to Pierce's Place or a little further to Novotny's. One advertisement stated "Nearest Hotel to the Insane Asylum."

+ Bernard "Bun" Brady purchased the business around 1940, renaming the business Brady's Bar. It was more commonly known as "Bun Brady's."

+ The building was badly damaged by fire in 1988, but renovated and restored to look much as it did in the early days.

GOING OUT OF THE
PHOTO BUSINESS
SPECIAL INDUCEMENTS UNTIL JUNE 30

- Joseph Maxbauer and his sons operated a meat market at another location in the early 1900s. Returning from World War I in 1919, Albert and Tony purchased Harvey Pierce's Saloon at 407 S. Union Street. Their goal was to open a meat market with all-new, modern processing equipment.

- The brothers became well known for their hot dogs and sausages. This tradition of quality remains today. The market closed during World War II, but continued the tradition afterwards.

- In 1964 the brothers sold the market to Barney and Tom Deering. The old wooden building was demolished and replaced with a Bavarian-style market. It was later sold to Mike Deering.

- In 2013 the market was sold to Marty Wilson.

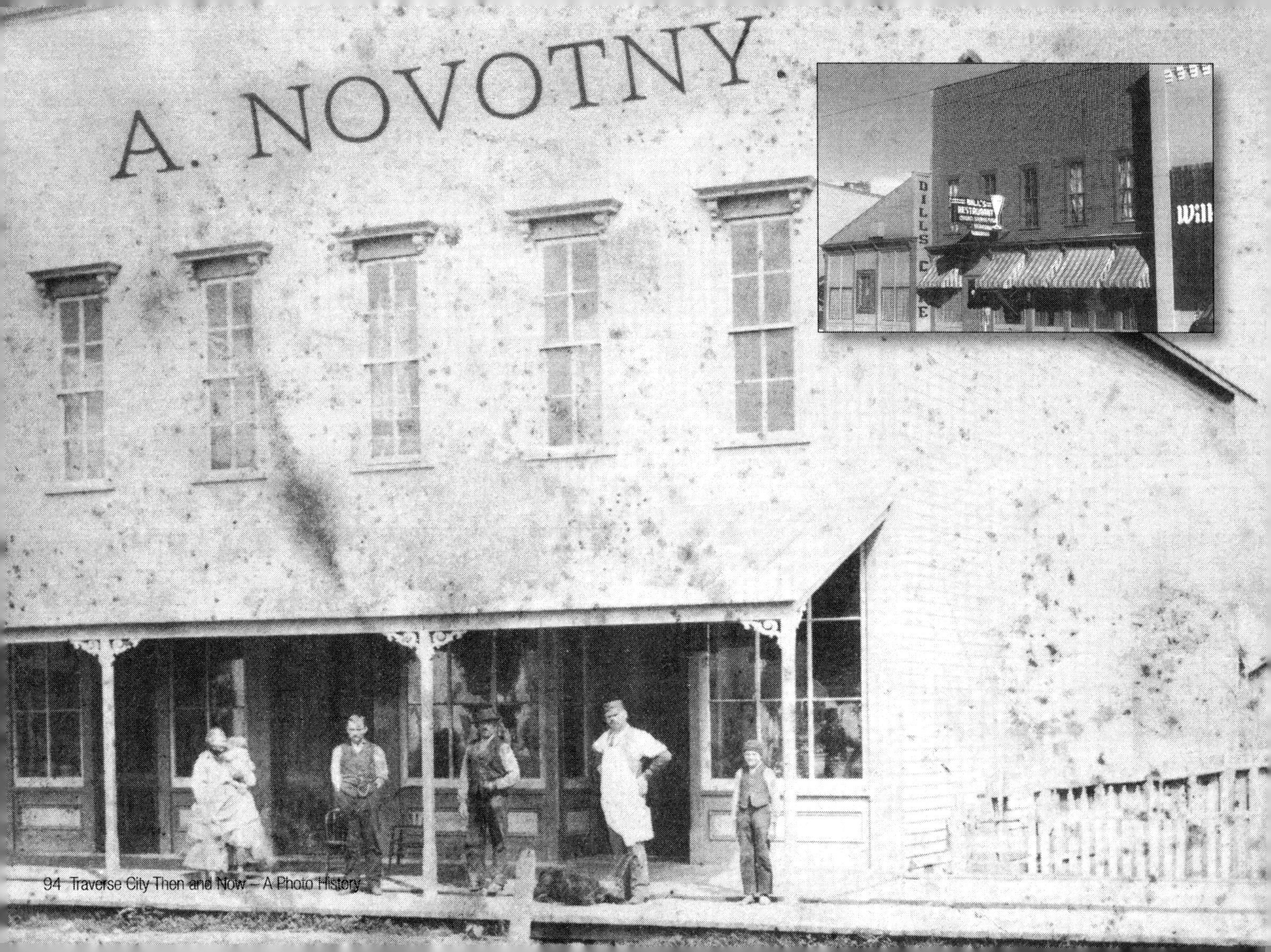
A. NOVOTNY
DILLS
RESTAURANT

- Antoine Novotny built his saloon and meat market in 1886. Besides being a drinking spot for the "young bucks," this became the south side social center. Except for the ladies of the Salvation Army passing the tambourine, no woman ever set foot inside. The headquarters for the Salvation Army was on the second floor.

- Next door to the saloon was Novotny's meat market. Each autumn the Bohemian boys would gather for a sauerkraut bee. Each man had a specified duty – a head cutter, a relief man and the chemist who fed the salt between the layers of cut cabbage. As the men worked, beer was given to them. One relief man cut off the end of his thumb, ruining fourteen gallons of good kraut.

- In 1939 William Dill purchased the business and the name changed to Dill's Café. On April 22, 1978 fire destroyed the original frame building. A replica was constructed in ten weeks. Several changes of ownership and remodeling occurred. Today the site is the Blue Tractor and Shed restaurants.

- In 1978 Novotny's was named a state historical site.

✦ A. J. Wilhelm owned a vacant brick store at the corner of Union and Eighth streets. It was built as a millinery shop for his sister but she left town and married a railroad executive before it ever opened.

✦ At the urging of the Bohemian neighborhood, A. J. and his brother Emanuel opened a clothing and dry goods store in1886.

✦ After one hundred years, three family generations and numerous remodelings the state historic landmark business and building closed in 1986.

✦ Since, the building has housed a restaurant, a furniture store and AT&T offices.

SOUTH SIDE CATHOLIC SCHOOL, TRAVERSE CITY, MICH.

✣ St. Francis School (also called the South Side Catholic School) was built in 1893 under the pastorage of Father Joseph Bauer. There were four classrooms on the main floor and two classrooms and a larger room on the second floor. By 1898 there were 300 students in grades 1 through 12 in seven classrooms. In 1913 a red brick gymnasium was constructed bordering Eleventh Street. A new gymnasium opened on November 26, 1954 and immediately saw the St. Francis basketball team defeat St. Mary's 41 to 30. With completion of the current St. Francis High School in 1966, the old school was demolished, replaced by a parking lot at Eleventh and Cass. On the last day the students marched to the tune of "Oh When the Saints Go Marching In" as they moved to the new school.

✢ The Union Street Elementary School was built on Union Street in 1905 to serve the south side of the city. There were eight classrooms. The school closed in the 1950s and was demolished soon after.

✢ On February 22, 1976 the parishioners of Saint Francis Church voted to build a new church on this site. It was consecrated by Bishop Edmund Szoka on November 6, 1977. Historic continuity was preserved by refurbishing and transferring four bells from the previous church and by transferring a document written by Rev. Theopole Nyssen from the cornerstone of the former church into the new one.

+ In the early 1900s the day of the livery barns along State Street were numbered. Dealers and repair shops for the "horseless carriage" were opening. In 1908, at the southeast corner of Cass and State Streets, the Wm. R. Goode Auto Garage opened. He advertised "Repairing, Vulcanization, Accessories and Sundries."

+ In 1928 Farrant and Sebright operated Dodge and Graham Bros. sales. In 1937 Northern Auto Body Service, operated by Edward Hockstad and Oscar Johnson, opened. Ole Westland had a used car lot across the street. During World War II, there was no business.

+ By 1945 M. J. MacIntosh moved his Mac's Service from E. Front Street to this location. In 1948 M. J. MacIntosh Oldsmobile, Cadillac and GMC was established with M. T. MacIntosh as president and Maxwell Crandall as vice-president. In 1958 Frank G. Paulos, a dealer for Cadillac and Oldsmobile, purchased the dealership. In 1964 Chet Swanson purchased the business.

+ On July 6, 1972 the *Record-Eagle* reported, "A fire roared through the Chet Swanson Cadillac Oldsmobile dealership at 202 E. State Street Thursday afternoon destroyed the block long structure containing two new automobiles and nine others being serviced." Swanson built a new dealership on Garfield Avenue.

+ The site was empty until the City Centre Plaza office building was built. Today Blue Care Network and the Towne Plaza restaurant are in that building.

✛ In 1873 a stagecoach line owned by Henry Campbell built the fifty-room Campbell Hotel at the southeast corner of State and Park Streets. In 1879 the hotel was sold to Hannah Lay and renamed the Park Place Hotel. A year later a 60-room annex was built at the southwest corner of State and Park Streets.

✛ R. Floyd Clinch, son-in-law of Tracy Lay, replaced the wooden hotel with a nine-floor brick tower in 1930. The original annex was torn down in the early 1950s. Eugene Power purchased and renovated the hotel in 1965. A year later a three-floor, 60-room addition, a convention dome and a swimming pool were added. In 1981, Power sold the renovated hotel to an out-of-state company.

✛ With major financial and management problems, the hotel was put up for sale. In October 1989 the Rotary Club of Traverse City purchased it. On Labor Day 1990 the hotel closed for an $8.5 million renovation. Today the state historical landmark stands successful and proud.

CHERRY COUNTY
PLAYHOUSE

ORSON BEAN
SEND ME NO FLOWERS

PLEASE
HELP KEEP
YOUR CITY
CLEAN

- In the summer of 1955 Ruth Bailey opened Cherry County Playhouse. For its first ten years shows were in a "circus-like" tent to the north across the street from the Park Place Hotel.

- Many popular comedies and dramas played. Stars of movies and television had lead roles: Buddy Ebsen, Imogene Coca, Soupy Sales and Burt Reynolds all performed there during the twenty-year run of the playhouse.

- After ten years the Playhouse moved across the street to the Park Place dome. In 1975 comedian Pat Paulson and partners purchased the theater. It closed in 1990 when a new theater site was not available in Traverse City. The theater company later moved to Muskegon.

- In 2004 a modern four-story office building was opened on the site of the original tent, but the memories remain.

- There were several livery stables along State Street including European Horse Hotel and B. J. Morgan's. Germaine Brothers sat across from the Park Place Hotel, one of the few brick structures on State Street. This location later became the site for several automobile dealers including Burns and Wyncoop, the local Chevrolet dealer.

- Today it is the site of the first downtown parking deck, named in honor of Larry Hardy, longtime city commissioner.

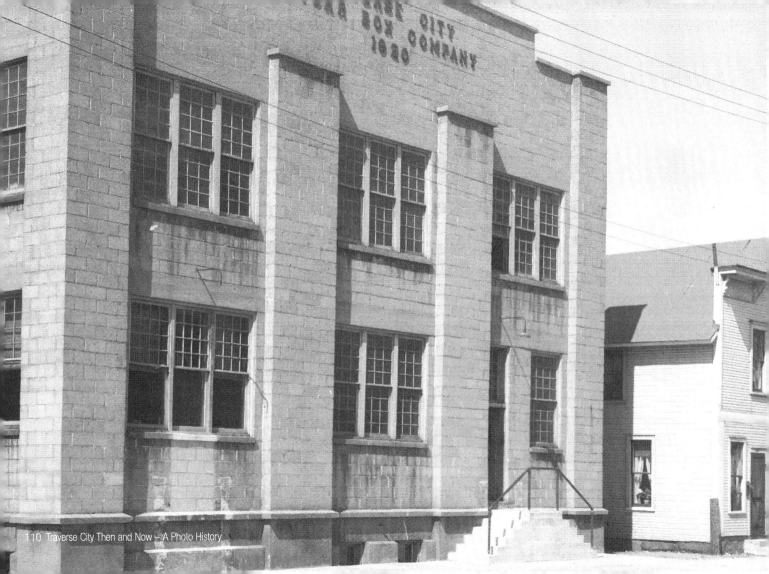

- Cigar manufacturing was a major Traverse City industry in the early twentieth century. Old Town was the location of several manufacturers, some of which were located in homes. John Furtsch operated a factory at 406 South Union. The building dates to 1883 and Furtsch manufactured cigars there until his death in 1911.

- At the corner of Sixth and Union Streets Frank L. Shuter made six brands of cigars. His brands ranged from the higher-priced Monarchs and Panatellas to Shuter's "Five Cent Brand."

- Alfred W. Jahraus cigar manufacturer and dealer was located at 214 E. Front. A cigar store Indian statue stood in front of this business for many years.

- The Traverse City Cigar Box Factory was constructed in 1921 at the corner of E. Eighth Street and Boardman Avenue. It replaced an older structure next door. As the days of cigar manufacturing declined, new businesses, including and furniture store and physical fitness facility occupied this building. Matt and Victoria Sutherland purchased the building in 2013.

+ In the early 1900s many towns hosted small hospitals. In Traverse City, Bay Bank Hospital operated from 1913 to 1921. Cook's Private Hospital was located at 733 Second Street. The Grand Traverse Hospital (also known as Shelternook) opened in 1901 near the corner of M22 and M-72. It burned in the spring of 1915.

+ Dr. Guy Johnson, MD, a staff physician at the State Hospital, opened the Johnson Hospital at the corner of State and Wellington streets in the 1920s. Dr. Johnson was Chief of Staff and Fleming Carrell was Assistant Physician. Other former State Hospital physicians served on the staff. In the early 1930s the hospital closed. The lumber from the demolished hospital was used to build the five stucco house which remain today at the corner of State and Wellington.

5,07.

- Washington Street became known as "Saint's Rest" after Perry Hannah donated property for several churches.

- Two churches were joined to form a modern government building.

- The eastern part of this complex was originally the Congregational Church, built in 1905 to replace its wooden predecessor. In 1961 members built a new church at the base of Old Mission Peninsula, and Bethany Baptist Church purchased the building.

- The western part of today's complex was built as a Presbyterian church, later becoming the Salvation Army building.

- Today, the building complex forms the Robert P. Griffin Hall of Justice, named in honor of the former U.S. Senator and Michigan Supreme Court Justice. It is now the District Court and the Probate and Family Court for Grand Traverse County. The Justice Center opened in 2006.

+ In 1908 State Senator James T. Milliken and his wife Hildegarde built this residence at the corner of Washington and Wellington Streets. James T. Milliken was the son of James W. Milliken, founder of Milliken Department Store. Mrs. Milliken was the daughter of Charles T. Grawn, Superintendent of Schools. This house was the boyhood home of Governor William Milliken.

+ At one time it served as the Rectory for Grace Episcool Church. Today it is a private residence.

✛ Grace Episcopal parish, organized in 1873 is one of the four oldest congregations in Traverse City. In July 1876 ground was broken on a thirty-foot lot on State Street. This was located next door to the European Horse Hotel livery. Because of the odor the parish sought a new site. Perry Hannah gave the parish $2000 so they could move the building to a larger plot at Boardman and Washington. James C. Morgan of Chicago, a partner of Hannah & Lay, gave financial aid to move the church. After 128 years, the building was old, crowded and the narthex needed to be replaced. In 2004 the membership voted to replace the past with a new, but similar, $1.9 million building.

- S. E. Wait was a true renaissance man. In the winter of 1851, he taught school aboard the original schooner "Madeline." He later operated the Pioneer Drug Store in the Masonic Building.

- He also was a meteorologist, tracking the weather of Northern Michigan for the Smithsonian and a skilled photographer.

- His house was built about 1870. After a disastrous fire, his home on Washington Street in the historic Boardman neighborhood has been restored.

- The Classical Revival Georgian home, designed by George L. Stone of Grand Rapids, was completed in 1908.

- He started construction of a Classical Revival Georgian home in 1905, and it was completed in 1908. The family lived in the home for only eight years. In 1916 the area's supply of hardwood lumber was depleted. The company and both Hull families moved to Tupper Lake, New York. The house was vacant for two years. It was then sold two times in two years. In 1929 the Sly Brothers purchased the home and converted it into two apartments.

- In 1989 the current owners bought the property and began a major renovation. The house had suffered years of neglect with severe water damage and foundation problems. The owners were advised to tear it down. Instead, after four years and what to many seemed like a miracle, the home became the Wellington Inn — an elegant bed and breakfast.

ESTABLISHED 1897
A.L. JOYCE
OLD RELIABLE BOTTLER
DEALER IN BAR
GLASSWARE AND SUPPLIES
Coca-Cola

+ A. L. Joyce opened his shop featuring "Old Reliable Bottler, Dealers in Bar and Glassware and Supplies" in 1897. He held contracts for several national carbonated beverages including Coca-Cola, plus locally produced items including Godelle Ginger Ale (in competition with Vernors), and Cherry Sparkler.

+ In 1920 Fred, Cyprian and Quincy Boughey purchased A. L. Joyce's business. Soon the Boughey Bottling truck could be seen throughout the area. They had the franchise brand for R.C. Cola, Squirt and Nehi. Diet Rite was the first diet cola on the market.

+ Boughey was sold in the 1960s and when it closed it brought to an end another pioneer business. The building is now a retail establishment.

TRAVERSE COUNTY CIVIC

+ In 1882 the land east of Garfield Street on Front Street was purchased by Frank and Nellie Desmond. Eighteen years later the land was sold to the Traverse City Driving Park Association for $4,000. It was used for harness racing. In 1905 the Driving Park land was sold to Howard and Isabelle Whiting. In 1912 the Whitings sold the land to Grand Traverse County for $10,000.

+ In 1912 the fair was moved from the Circus Grounds to the Driving Park site. For the next sixth-two years the Northwestern Michigan Fair showcased agriculture, homemaking and horticulture. The last fair at this site was in 1974. In 1975 the fair was moved to Blair Townhall Road.

+ With a $50,000 federal grant and a matching state grant from a recreation bond, the development of the Grand Traverse Civic Center began. Today the Civic Center has developed into a major recreation area. The swimming pool and the adjoining Howe Arena are highlights. Baseball fields, tennis courts, a playground and a skate park have been built. A pavilion on the southwest corner provides for an entertainment center. A walking trail around the park is well used, as are the other features.

- In 2012 Traverse City was designated the 10th Coast Guard City in the United States. The Coast Guard's current headquarters has been home to military installations since the early 1940s.

- The Coast Guard considered placing a facility here as early as 1941, but did not stay in the area. A permanent military presence can be traced to 1942 when the U.S. Navy arrived to conduct "secret" projects with remote-controlled aircraft, or drones. This was the beginning of guided missile research.

- The Navy had converted two palatial passenger ships to "faux" aircraft carriers, which were driven by two huge paddle wheels. At least one of these was used on Grand Traverse Bay in connection with drone research.

- The Navy left the air base on November 15, 1945 and transferred the property to the Coast Guard.

Other Books About Traverse City

The Traverse City State Hospital Training School for Nurses, *by Virginia M. LeClaire (May 4, 2012)*

Traverse City, Michigan: A Historical Narrative, 1850-2013, *by Richard Fidler (2012)*

Glimpses of Grand Traverse Past: Reflections on a Local History, *by Richard Fidler (June 2, 2008)*

Who We Were, What We Did: Fresh Perspectives on Grand Traverse History, *by Richard Fidler (2009)*

Gateways to Grand Traverse Past, *by Richard Fidler (2011)*

Edgewood Resort A Place Apart, *by Julie A. Schopieray (2011)*

Grand Traverse Legends Volume I: The Early Years 1838-1860, *by Robert E. Wilson (2004)*

Grand Traverse Legends Volume II: The Formative Years 1860-1880, *by Robert E. Wilson (2005)*

Grand Traverse Legends Volume III: The Transition Years 1880-1900, *by Robert E. Wilson (2006)*

Grand Traverse Journal, *Locally-produced digital magazine featuring nature and local history from the Grand Traverse Region. http://gtjournal.tadl.org/*

Perry Hannah's Gifts, *by Peg Jonkhoff & Fred Hoisington (2013)*

Bibliography

Anderson, W.S., *Old settlers Association of the Grand Traverse Region, 1925*

Archives of the Author

Archives of the History Center of Traverse City

Faith and Knowledge: The History of the Grand Traverse Catholic Schools

Fidler, Richard, *Gateway to Grand Traverse Past*

Polk Directories, Assorted volumes 1900-1990

Preview Community Weekly

Traverse City Record-Eagle

Wakefield, Larry, *Grand Old Lady: The Story of the Traverse City Opera House*

Wakefield, Larry, *Historic Traverse City Houses*

Wilson, Robert, *Grand Traverse Legends, Vol. 1*

Wilson, Robert, *Grand Traverse Legends, Vol. 2*

44889798R00079

Made in the USA
San Bernardino, CA
25 January 2017